formatio

TRADITION. EXPERIENCE.
TRANSFORMATION.

Formatio books from InterVarsity Press follow the rich tradition of the church in the journey of spiritual formation. These books are not merely about being informed, but about being transformed by Christ and conformed to his image. Formatio stands in InterVarsity Press's evangelical publishing tradition by integrating God's Word with spiritual practice and by prompting readers to move from inward change to outward witness. InterVarsity Press uses the chambered nautilus for Formatio, a symbol of spiritual formation because of its continual spiral journey outward as it moves from its center. We believe that each of us is made with a deep desire to be in God's presence. Formatio books help us to fulfill our deepest desires and to become our true selves in light of God's grace.

 Spiritual Formation for Individuals and Groups

SOUL SEARCHING

MINDY CALIGUIRE

IVP Connect

An imprint of InterVarsity Press
Downers Grove, Illinois

InterVarsity Press
P.O. Box 1400, Downers Grove, IL 60515-1426
World Wide Web: www.ivpress.com
E-mail: email@ivpress.com

InterVarsity Press® is the book-publishing division of InterVarsity Christian Fellowship/ USA®, a student movement active on campus at hundreds of universities, colleges and schools of nursing in the United States of America, and a member movement of the International Fellowship of Evangelical Students. For information about local and regional activities, write Public Relations Dept., InterVarsity Christian Fellowship/USA, 6400 Schroeder Rd., P.O. Box 7895, Madison, WI 53707-7895, or visit the IVCF website at <www.intervarsity.org>.

All Scripture quotations, unless otherwise indicated, are taken from the Holy Bible, Today's New International Version™ Copyright © 2001 by International Bible Society. All rights reserved.

Design: Cindy Kiple
Images: LWA/Getty Images

ISBN 978-0-8308-3521-8

Printed in the United States of America ∞

P 20 19 18 17 16 15 14 13 12 11 10 9 8 7 6 5 4 3 2 1

Y 24 23 22 21 20 19 18 17 16 15 14 13 12 11 10 09 08

CONTENTS

INTRODUCTION
Who Are You?

I approached the children's ministry table that Sunday morning, eager to meet the volunteers who would welcome my son Josh into his new classroom. I kept Josh beside me so he could meet the women at the registration table and, with my hands on his shoulders, introduced him: "This is Joshua Caliguire." The woman directly in front of Josh dutifully began to write out his name tag and sign him into the class, but the woman next to her looked up at me with great anticipation and asked, "Do you know Mindy Caliguire?"

"Excuse me?" I asked, thinking I had misunderstood the question. But immediately, she looked at me and asked again, "Do you know Mindy Caliguire?"

When she asked the second time, I paused and stepped back a bit, not knowing where this conversation would go. She filled in the airspace, explaining, "The reason I ask is that I just finished taking a five-week class on membership that she taught *[yes, that I taught]*, and it was a great class. But it's such an unusual name I thought you might be related!"

At this point I really didn't know what was going on, but since my son was in this class for the next year, I figured I had to come clean at some point, so I said, "I hate to tell you, but I *am* Mindy Caliguire."

"Oh, I'm sorry I didn't recognize you," she said. "You look so much younger at a distance!"

She clapped her hand over her mouth when she realized what she had said! We both laughed hysterically, though internally I wondered, *Where will I find a plastic surgeon nearby? How can I teach from greater and greater distances?* But beyond my slightly bruised ego, the question "Do you know Mindy Caliguire?" lingered in my mind for quite some time. I finally realized why.

I used to hear that question from the woman who looks back at me in the mirror each morning. When I stopped hurrying and scurrying long enough, the sad whispers could be heard: *Do you know Mindy Caliguire? Do you know what makes her laugh? Cry? Do you know what she dreams about? What she's afraid of?*

The truth about me in that season was that I had completely lost touch with the person God made me to be. My soul was in trouble—it was crying out, but I refused to heed its call. I wasn't sure the answers to those questions even mattered. Weren't we supposed to die to ourselves in serving God? Does it really matter who Mindy Caliguire is?

It turns out it does. But I realized it too late; my soul, neglected and ignored as it was, crashed and burned. In that struggle and the time of healing that followed, though, I made a crucial discovery: the abundant life Jesus promised comes when we know ourselves and serve others from the truest parts of who we are.

Many people, I find, face a similar struggle with their identity and with the well-being of their soul. They can relate to the idea of losing themselves *in the wrong way* right in the middle of their own lives.

Perhaps you've been through a similar season—or that's the very question you asked yourself just this morning. No matter your story, I hope that you will find this book to be a valuable resource in your spiritual journey. Entering into the process of soul searching can do much to recover life and health for the soul.

Soul searching is hardly new, of course. It has a long history through various Christian traditions, under several names. During the 1400s, the Jesuits within the Catholic Church began the practice of "self-examination" or "examen," which became a mainstay for a deepening spiritual experience. In the 1700s Quakers prized the soul-searching practice of silence, often accompanied by "queries" or "questions of the soul" posed to the self for reflection. Even today, secular twelve-step communities, rooted in Christian theology and practice, urge a process of ongoing soul searching among adherents.

What difference did it make? The Jesuits surmounted the corruption of the institutional church in their day and paved a new path for intimacy and service. The Quakers, though a small and quiet sect, pioneered Christian renunciation of slavery, freeing their own slaves—forfeiting fortunes—and offering historic assistance to build the underground railroad. And in an underground movement of a different kind, former addicts humbly illuminate a path of rescue from self-destruction to life.

That very same life-giving, strengthening, transformational power awaits you, today, whatever your need. I think if those who have gone ahead on the journey could speak to us, they would say, "Don't settle! Don't settle for an unlived life!"

Don't give in to lukewarm spiritual climates near you, to the godless culture surrounding you, to the temptations within you. The power to rise above these will not come from your own resources, but can only be known and received in the deepest parts of your soul—not your soul as it should or could be, but as it actually is.

"What good will it be for you to gain the whole world, yet forfeit your soul?" (Matthew 16:26). There is no good whatsoever in gaining anything at the expense of your soul. Don't settle. Face what needs to be faced, receive what you need to receive, let go of whatever you need to let go of . . . and live.

The Path of Soul Care

Soul Care Resources are designed to offer a simple, but not simplistic, guide to maintaining or recovering the life and health of your soul, that essential personhood created by God as *you*.

This book is divided into four experiences. Within each experience are four distinct parts that could be used as daily readings. Some parts are longer than others, so feel free to take more than a day to cover the material. Each part builds on the other, so you'll want to read one part at a time and reflect on the questions embedded in the text.

If daily readings aren't workable for you, just spending a day or two with each of the parts should allow you to comfortably complete one experience in a week, and the entire guide within about a month.

The fifth section of each part includes a discussion starter that you can use with a small group or friend if you wish.

As you muster the intentionality and reach out toward God in trust, you will most certainly find soul searching to be both life-giving and soul-healing. In essence, you'll find what David found to be true: "He refreshes my soul" (Psalm 23:3).

"Men go abroad to wonder at the heights
of mountains, at the huge waves of the sea,
at the long courses of the rivers, at the vast
compass of the ocean, at the circular motions
of the stars, and they pass by themselves
without wondering."

ST. AUGUSTINE, *CONFESSIONS*

EXPERIENCE ONE / *Embarking on a Brave Journey*

1 PEERING WITHIN

The journey we're embarking on starts with a specific question: what exactly is soul searching as a spiritual practice?

Our answer is especially important because one of the greatest potential dangers in this practice can be avoided if the definition of soul searching is truly understood and heeded. As you'll soon see, the very real temptation to deviate from a very simple idea produces devastating results.

■ As you consider the idea of intentional soul searching, what do you most look forward to? What do you most resist?

■ Take the remaining space provided to speak directly to God about
your hopes and concerns.

Soul searching *is an honest look inside, guided by the Holy Spirit.*
Psalm 139:23-24 gives us a clear picture of the heart-cry of someone correctly moving into a time of soul searching. In this psalm, the
writer, Israel's beloved King David, implores:

Search me, God, and know my heart;
   test me and know my anxious thoughts.
See if there is any offensive way in me,
   and lead me in the way everlasting.

A paraphrased translation reads:

Investigate my life, O God,
   find out everything about me;
Cross-examine and test me,
   get a clear picture of what I'm about;
See for yourself whether I've done anything wrong—
   then guide me on the road to eternal life.
(Psalm 139:23-24 The Message)

14

■ Which part of that prayer do you most resonate with today? Why?

■ Which part would be the most difficult for you to honestly pray? Why?

Richard Foster's book *Celebration of Discipline* outlines two distinct and very different categories of soul searching, which he refers to by the classical term *self-examination,* or prayers of examen. The distinction between these two classical forms of soul searching centers on two very important parts of our interior world: our conscience (moral navigation and recording) and our consciousness (or awareness) of God. While many of us are mindful of the conscience, the concept of examining our day-to-day or even moment-by-moment awareness (or consciousness) of God is often a new challenge.

■ How aware are you, typically, of your "conscience"? Under what circumstances are you most sensitive to your conscience?

When have you sensed your conscience guiding you or warning you?

■ How would you describe your typical level of "consciousness" or awareness of God's presence and activity in your life?

I usually enter into this soul searching process by writing in my journal—often beginning an entry with the word "Yesterday . . ." and then inviting God to remind me of those things that were important to record and, when necessary, to resolve or reconcile.

These soul-searching prayers help me become more conscious of the active part God plays during ordinary days, even if I had been unaware of God's presence in the moment. Prayerful reflection on the prior day helps me see God's presence at times I had not felt it, and over time it has helped me grow in my ability to sense God's presence with me at all times. The more aware of God's presence I become, the more likely I am to seek guidance, willingly choose what's best and right, and experience the peace that surpasses understanding no matter what else is going on.

■ What difference might an increased awareness of God on a daily basis make in your life?

■ What would you hope your awareness of God could be like in ordinary moments (like right now)? What physical object could symbolize that vision or desire? (This could be light on a path, rushing water or a growing vine—or something less "biblical" like an electrical cord or whatever you come up with!) Take a few minutes to find something and put it in a place where you'll see it frequently, or draw a picture of that image here.

The three core elements of soul searching as a spiritual practice are these:

- The *location* of the investigation—the *interior* of one's life, or the soul

- The *nature* of the investigation—in this case, one that is *honest*

- The *leader* of the investigation—God, and *only God*

All three elements in the list above are important for soul searching to be experienced as a life-giving, soul-building and transformational process. Also of particular importance is the ability to correctly discern the voice of God. Soul searching is not a "superspiritual" or "elite" practice, but it does require a measure of humility and discernment, both typically developed over time in a growing relationship with God. You don't need to wait until some magical moment to start, though. By simply engaging the process, discernment and humility will be honed and developed.

Without the above elements, soul searching can quickly devolve, not just to something irrelevant or impotent, but to a process that can be downright discouraging or even destructive. Perhaps because of that possibility—we'll call it "soul searching gone wrong"—many people resist and avoid this spiritual practice altogether. They are wise not to continue something harmful, but with some gentle coaching and proper emphasis, the process can be embraced with great confidence.

How might soul searching go wrong? Let's begin by considering what happens when we take a *dishonest* look inside, guided by the *self.*

The human propensity for self-serving bias is well known and researched. The Bible clearly conveys this idea too, as in Jeremiah 17:9: "The heart is deceitful above all things / and beyond cure. / Who can understand it?" Sounds a bit dark, huh? When the self leads the process of soul searching, the result is a dishonest appraisal of the interior life.

What does the sometimes dishonest, self-seeking self see inside? Nothing but goodness and purity. The extreme example would be the diagnosable pathology in mental health, a personality disorder known as narcissism. But the temptation to narcissistic thinking is common to all of us; we put ourselves at the center of our own universe. A look inside becomes dishonest when we gaze only upon our better qualities and ignore our own shortcomings and wrongful choices. Clearly if we look inside and fail to see the truth about ourselves there, the soul searching will never reach its target. It is soul searching gone wrong.

C. S. Lewis possessed amazing creativity and insight into the human soul, particularly into our ability to ignore certain truths about ourselves. One very humorous but poignant example of this comes from *The Screwtape Letters,* in which Lewis imagines a series of letters from the demon Screwtape to his protégé, Wormwood. Through the letters, Screwtape counsels Wormwood in his task of keeping his "patient," a man, out of the grips of the Enemy (who would be God!).

Read Screwtape's "advice" below as it relates to soul searching (self-examination). Keep in mind that there's a complete inversion of good and evil!

My Dear Wormwood,

I am very pleased by what you tell me about this man's relations with his mother. But you must press your advantage. The Enemy will be working from the center outwards, gradually bringing more and more of the patient's conduct under the new standard, and may reach his behavior to the old lady at any moment. You want to get in first. Keep in close touch with our colleague Glubose who is in charge of the mother, and build up between you in that house a good settled habit of mutual annoyance: daily pinpricks. The following methods are useful.

1. Keep his mind on his inner life. He thinks his conversion [to Christianity] is something inside him and his attention is therefore chiefly turned at present to the states of his own mind—or rather to that very expurgated version of them which is all you should allow him to see. Encourage this. Keep his mind off the most elementary duties by directing it to the most advanced and spiritual ones. Aggravate that most useful human characteristic, the horror and neglect of the obvious. You must bring him to a condition in which he can practice self-examination for an hour without discovering any of those facts about himself which are perfectly clear to anyone who has ever lived with him or worked in the same office. *(p.10, emphasis mine)*

Elsewhere Screwtape advises, "You may ask whether it is possible to keep such an obvious thought from occurring even to a human mind. It is, Wormwood, it is! Handle him properly and it simply won't come into his head. He has not been anything like long enough with the Enemy to have any real humility yet" (p. 14).

Left to our own devices, we can do the very thing Lewis describes—spend time in soul searching but completely miss the truth about ourselves.

■ When have you witnessed someone's (or your own) refusal to see truth about themselves? In what way do you imagine that affected their (or your) spiritual development?

3 GUIDED BY THE HOLY SPIRIT

We are not capable of leading the process of soul searching on our own. Who is wise enough to help us see what's really going on inside the soul? Only God can see with full clarity and, like a wise physician, guide us in the direction of healing, into truth and light. We need to be willing both to let him lead our searching and to listen for his divine interpretation of what the soul search reveals.

I once taught a class that included some hearing-impaired participants and an interpreter to sign for them. While I spoke, I noticed the effortless way the students' attention remained fixed primarily on their interpreter—not on me. None of them had to be reminded to pay attention to the interpreter during each point because they knew they couldn't learn the material correctly without the interpreter's help. Perhaps when the students were younger and first using an interpreter they were frustrated that they couldn't understand what was being said without assistance. But now, in my class, joyfully signing to each other and the interpreter, they politely ignored me, the teacher. Instead, they effortlessly turned their focus toward the interpreter, who willingly and efficiently signed the correct information to them.

In a similar way, we need God's divine interpretation to understand our soul correctly. Without his guidance, we may move in absurd directions or draw absurd conclusions. In fact, there's actually a connection between not hearing (especially when it comes to our relationship with God!) and absurdity. The Latin word for deaf is *surdis,* and it's the root word for the English "absurd." Perhaps you've used that word within the last month to describe your own life! When we have lost our ability to hear and understand what's really going on around us, our lives can become absurd.

When we practice soul searching under the guidance of our own spirit, rather than God's, we run two dangers: not only do we face the absurdity of not hearing the truth, but we struggle to do the right thing even if we happen to discern it. We can't *hear* well, and we can't *do* well.

Again, a Latin word—*audire*—furthers our understanding. You'll likely recognize many words in the English language that come from this root word—*auditory, auditorium, audition*—all referencing the ability to hear. But another English word also comes from *audire:* "obey." It's not as easy a connection for us to see, but in fact, the ideas are so closely linked that some Old Testament passages show "hear" and "obey" translated alternately for the same root word.

■ How would you describe the link between hearing and obedience?

■ Can you think of a time in your life when obedience to God flowed naturally from a clear understanding of what God has said, or said specifically to you in a particular situation?

In addition to not listening to God, soul searching can go wrong when we take an honest look inside, guided by the *self.* This form of soul searching lurks at the other end of the spectrum from taking a dishonest look inside. It is slightly more virtuous, perhaps, in its willingness to face the sometimes-ugly truths inside, but it's no less harmful to the soul because the self is still not a trustworthy guide.

■ Notice the time on a clock near you right now. Give yourself no more than two minutes for this exercise—be careful to watch! Writing whatever comes to mind, quickly list as many things about yourself that are imperfect (unhealthy habits, true failures, frustrating addictions, brash selfishness, whatever comes to mind).

All too often, ignoring our limitations, we attempt soul searching on our own—with our own spirit leading the way. This is disastrous on many levels. The temptation for some of us is to enter into a full-fledged witch-hunt (complete with burnings) on the self; we look within and only see the parts of us that we hate or reject. Especially if you are a perfectionist by nature, the practice of soul searching can fill entire pages of a journal with lists of shortcomings, flaws and failures. God is conspicuously absent from this process.

How long did it take you to list your imperfections and flaws? I'm guessing not long. My point is not to question whether your list is true or not; most of us have at least a hint of the areas in which we're stuck and hurting ourselves and/or others. Rather, the point is this: you are more than capable of making such a list, but the process was not specifically *led* by the Holy Spirit. Nothing on that list tells you which area in your life God would like you to particularly pay attention to right now, or which area God is most concerned about for your next step on the journey.

You may decide to emphasize one thing, when in fact *the Spirit* would have led you differently, knowing what's best. And when you lack God's leadership, the temptation will be to further craft some master plan for spiritual growth—in your own strength. Though motivated by areas that do need change, self-improvement efforts, even in spiritual matters, generally do not produce freedom and life. If they succeed, we become prideful in our ability to grow. If they fail, we become disheartened and discouraged. Either way, both the desired change and the path pursued to achieve it were determined without God.

Return to Psalm 139:23-24 below. Prayerfully work through each phrase and make this prayer your own.

Search me, God, and know my heart;
*   test me and know my anxious thoughts.*
See if there is any offensive way in me,
*   and lead me in the way everlasting.*

Feel free to go back to that list you made and scratch it all off, erase it, or tear the page out and burn it!

For those who are led by the Spirit of God are the children of God.
(Romans 8:14)

Often in the Bible, when God spoke to his people, there was no
ambiguity about what was being said or about who was speaking.
Whether they heard an out-loud voice or not (and I suspect they often
did), Moses, Abraham, Noah and many others responded to God's
voice in ordinary ways. They seemed to converse naturally with God.
In fact, in Exodus 33:11, we learn that "the Lord would speak to Moses
face to face, as one speaks to a friend."

But not everyone immediately recognized God's voice in ancient
days, just like many of us struggle to discern when he's speaking to us
today. The Old Testament prophet Samuel stands out as a refreshing
example of someone who didn't quite understand what was going on
when he first heard God speaking. Heeding his spiritual mentor, Eli,
Samuel eventually learned to recognize God's voice on his own. We
too can learn to recognize God's voice, and it will be very important
to do so as we enter times of soul searching.

But how? How might we learn to hear God's voice?

1. Study Scripture. The most important way to develop our capacity to hear God's voice is to become a diligent student of what God has already communicated—through the pages of Scripture. When we examine the Wisdom literature in the Scriptures, we come to better understand God's ways. When we study Jesus in the Gospels, we understand how he responds to us. But beyond learning what God has already revealed for instruction and growth, the pages of Scripture also reveal the *ways* God speaks and the *kinds* of things he tends to say to those who screw up, who stray, who choose to follow other gods. When we study the whole of Scripture, we understand the story of God among his people—the story that continues on today. We get to know God's heart, God's purposes, God's priorities and God's ways.*

■ How well do you know the Scriptures? What helped you learn?

■ What do you wish you had a better grasp of?

■ Are there gaping holes in your study? Where, and why might that be?

---

*A great resource for further study is Gordon Fee's *How to Read the Bible for All It's Worth.*

Personal Bible study also matters because God sometimes speaks directly to our hearts through an actual passage of Scripture. Somehow, the words speak to us even beyond what is written, as it seems to apply just to us—just at that time. This occurs because of the distinctly supernatural essence of the Bible. It's certainly no ordinary book of wisdom: "For the word of God is living and active. Sharper than any double-edged sword, it penetrates even to dividing soul and spirit, joints and marrow; it judges the thoughts and attitudes of the heart" (Hebrews 4:12).

■ Have you ever experienced this with the Bible?

■ What do you recall about that experience?

2. Enlist the help of an Eli. Like Samuel, we sometimes need another person's help in discerning the voice of God. During one time of soul searching, I shared with a trusted and spiritually mature friend the various things I sensed God saying to me. While I don't remember specifics, it involved the many "assignments" I felt God had given me to work on, both personal and work-related. Perhaps I shared my sense of feeling overwhelmed and somewhat exasperated, possibly at the "unfairness" of it all, but I remember my friend listening intently and, for the first time in my life, calling into question this voice I heard in my head—the voice I had always assumed to be the voice of God. "Mindy," she said, "it sounds like you serve a God of impossible demands." She helped me learn that God's voice is not one of shrill, strident, shaming demands.

The ability to hear God's voice is perhaps the most critical factor for effective soul searching. Enlisting the help of a spiritual director or friend would be a wise choice if you feel like you're hearing-impaired when it comes to God and direct communication.

■ Who helps, or has helped, you understand and respond to the voice of God?

Who could you ask to help you in the future?

3. Use a journal. Sometimes it helps to record the things you sense God saying in the pages of a journal. Naturally, you'll want to have a record of these things for future reference. But more importantly, especially in the process of learning to discern the voice of God, recording these words in a journal gives you the opportunity to objectively stand back from the experience of listening to God in order to prayerfully assess the words. Do they line up with the kinds of things God says in Scripture, or do they contradict God's previous revelation? Anything that contradicts the revelation in the Bible can't be from God.

■ When have you recorded something you sensed God communicating to you in the pages of a journal or somewhere else? How did the process of writing it down serve you, if at all?

■ Take some time to write down anything you sense God saying to you right now through this study (or something else current).

Mishearing the voice of God can leave us tired and joyless, especially if an internal tyrant becomes the voice of God. The internal tyrant says things like, *"If you really loved me, you would . . ."* And because we don't want our love for God called into question in any way, we salute smartly and do whatever that voice tells us. That definitely happened with me; my internal tyrant led me to believe that every opportunity to help someone else became my obligation to do so.

The internal tyrant also brings severe and ongoing condemnation for every sin, past and present. But as we gain discernment, we can recognize that condemnation is a dead giveaway that this is not the voice of God. Romans 8 assures us that there is no condemnation for those who are in Christ. As the Holy Spirit works in our hearts, he absolutely brings *conviction* when we choose something wrong—conviction, but not condemnation. God's kindness leads us to repentance, even though that may be very difficult to hear. Our conscience may be sensitized to the Spirit's conviction, but we are never crushed by condemnation from God.

■ As you consider moving into specific ways of soul searching, how confident are you in your ability to discern God's voice?

■ Which of these three listening lessons (studying the Scripture, enlisting the help of an Eli or using a journal) is the strongest for you? Which would interest you as a possible next step?

5 GROUP DISCUSSION

Summary

In the business of everyday life, many people struggle to maintain a healthy connection to their core identity, and soul searching is one spiritual practice that can help us connect authentically back with God—the source of our truest self. Some forms of soul searching explore our conscience, while others urge us to explore our consciousness, or awareness, of God. In either case, soul searching involves an honest look inside, guided by the Holy Spirit. Thus, it requires some time, effort and humility. But just as important, it requires an ability to discern the voice of God directing the process, because a focus on the self—without God's perspective, grace, direction and leadership—can hurt more than help. Each of us can grow in our capacity to hear God more clearly as we study the Scriptures, enlist the help of trusted friends, and prayerfully journal and reflect on anything we sense God may be saying. And God's words will always be consistent with God's loving character. As we are immersed in this profound and active love, we live into our truest identity.

Opening

What inspired your interest in this exploration of soul searching?

Discussion

1. What, if anything, did you sense God stirring in you through this first experience?

2. Go back over your written responses to parts one through four. What one or two ideas would you like to bring to the group?

3. Read Psalm 139:23-24. What kind of circumstances do you imagine would have led someone to compose such a psalm?

   When, if ever, has a similar prayer been the same desire of your heart?

4. Have you had an experience of God leading you specifically or personally? What happened? How did you know it was God?

5. Which of the ways to develop discernment is most natural or

appealing to you (studying the Scriptures, enlisting help from a friend or journaling)?

Which seems most difficult?

6. As you consider this entire study, what are you looking forward to?

What might you tend to resist?

Prayer

If you feel comfortable, have one or several group members close this time in prayer.

Before the next gathering, everyone should complete "Experience Two: Increasing Awareness of God."

"God is at home.
It is we who have gone out for a walk."

MEISTER ECKHART

EXPERIENCE TWO / *Increasing Awareness of God*

1 EXAMEN OF CONSCIOUSNESS

While some ways of soul searching are aimed specifically at the conscience, others direct their inquiry toward elevating our consciousness—our awareness—of God. So many responsibilities and people demand our attention—family and friends, work, errands, ministry—that's it's easy to walk through a day or even months largely unaware of God's presence and work. It takes intentionality on our part to grow in our awareness of him. That's where the spiritual practice of soul searching can serve our spiritual development.

Missing the Obvious

Turning away from God's ways in outright rebellion certainly diminishes our spiritual vitality. But losing connection to God due to distractions can squeeze the life from our souls as well—and, in contrast to rebellion, it can happen so subtly that we might not notice for days or weeks or months. Just as can occur with a close friend, we suddenly realize too much time has gone by since we meaningfully connected, and it just feels weird or maybe a little sad. We might wonder where God has been lately and how we start back. How do we develop a moment-to-moment relationship with God? Is it reasonable to hope for such a thing?

■ Have you ever felt a twinge of sadness over the loss of connection with a close friend?

With God?

What did you do to rectify the situation, if anything?

Read Luke 10:38-42 and answer the following questions.

■ Who do you most naturally identify with in this story, Martha or Mary? Why?

■ What current distractions pose the greatest threat to your ability to sense God, even when God is right there with you? (Keep in mind that these distractions may be perfectly fine things in and of themselves, such as a new educational endeavor or a new baby in the house!)

■ Read through the passage a second time, very slowly. Then a third time. What, if anything, do you sense God saying to you through this?

One of the best-known ways of developing our consciousness of God comes to us from the teaching and ministry of Ignatius of Loyola, a vocal reformer of the church in the 1400s. Under his teaching, a covenant community (the "society of Jesus") formed, known today within the Catholic Church as the Jesuits. Ignatius developed a rhythm of intentional prayer—a prayer of examen—to aid in rekindling and reconnecting our relationship with God day by day with the sure hope of transformation as a result.

I particularly love some of the fresh language related to this ancient form of prayer:

This small prayer, the Examen of Consciousness, is the heart of the spirituality developed by St. Ignatius Loyola and his followers. If practiced once or twice daily, it will help move you closer to the heart of Christ in all your thoughts and deeds. The point of it is to find the sources of unfreedom in your life—old habits, people, situations, conditions—that lead you to make cramped choices away from what would be God's will.

The more we notice how we can change and move toward God like flowers to the sun, the freer we become. As God continually labors within us to make us more like His Son, we can either cooperate with his unfolding creation or freely choose not to. The choice is ours, and, like the prophets, Ignatius reminds us to "Choose life!" (Phyllis Zagano, "Examen of Consciousness: Finding God in All Things")

"Unfreedom" and "cramped choices"—what great words! Those words help me put fresh language around the reality of sin in my soul, and they express the truth of how our souls feel when we choose other than God. When we learn to *sense* those feelings, we can more quickly recognize when we're moving away from God and then ask for God's help.

Key Steps in a Review

There are five steps to the examen of consciousness:

1. Recall you are in the presence of God.
2. Look at your day with gratitude.
3. Ask for help from the Holy Spirit.
4. Review your day.
5. Reconcile and resolve.

You'll notice that the bulk of the soul searching comes in parts four and five; the first three steps significantly set the tone and context for the examen. Steps one through three remind us of our context: "Search me, God, and know my heart; . . . lead me in the way everlasting." Even in prayer, these foundational truths and requests can be ignored or forgotten.

We will work through each aspect of the prayer of examen bit by bit. Eventually, you will be able to work through the five steps as a complete, whole experience. For now, let's explore the first one.

Recall You Are in the Presence of God

The gentle reminder of this first step helps us already with the very thing we're trying to do—become aware of God's presence with us at all times, which of course means right here, right now! You might find it helpful to meditate on Scripture passages that speak to this, such as Psalm 139 ("Where can I go from your Spirit?"), Matthew 28 ("I am with you always."), Romans 8 ("Who shall separate us from the love of Christ?") or Hebrews 13:5 ("Never will I leave you; never will I forsake you.").

Pause for a few minutes and do that right now. Acknowledge God's presence. Perhaps one or more of those Scriptures stood out. Perhaps the amazing truth of God's presence with you struck something deep inside. Is there something you'd like to communicate to God right now? Anything you sense God communicating to you?

■ Use the space provided to write a response to God. Take one of the Scriptures mentioned above and paraphrase it—writing it out here, using your own name, instead of "I" or "you," where appropriate.

Do a quick gut-check: did you notice anything change in your disposition, or even in your physical body, as you recalled that you are in the presence of God?

■ What difference do you expect it will make when you begin a time of soul searching mindful of God's presence?

2 GIVING THANKS AND ASKING FOR THE SPIRIT'S HELP

As we just learned, soul searching begins with awareness of God's presence. Now let's look together at the second and third steps.

Look at Your Day with Gratitude

The step of looking back with gratitude is not time-consuming. It's a matter of orientation, of putting in place a crucial perspective. Some people naturally see their lives and their days in light of God's goodness and love for them; others seriously struggle to achieve or maintain that perspective (authentically, that is). Regardless of our basic tendencies, this step is significant for all of us as we enter a time of soul searching. In it, we pause and choose the perspective of gratitude. Why would that matter?

It's possible to look back on our days, if we consider them at all, only with regret or disappointment. Our tendency toward self-orientation really drives these attitudes. As I learned about the prayer of examen from a Jesuit priest in my area, I was surprised to discover that even my times of self-recrimination—mentally rehearsing an unkind action or word I had spoken, accompanied by vows of self-improvement—revealed my self-orientation. Rather than looking back on a day with gratitude, I was filled only with self-absorbed remorse. At other times when I've looked back, I have been filled with disappointment in others or in circumstances, which is similarly self-referencing. None of those reflections acknowledges God. None of them draws me to see the day, even if filled with my own foolishness, as a gift from God. As long as I remain focused on myself, I'm the center of my own universe.

■ Think back to a recent time when you failed in some way. How did you respond?

■ Do you tend toward self-recrimination? How present is God to you during those times?

■ Now, consider a recent disappointment you suffered. How did that experience shift your sense of God's nearness, if at all?

Gratitude, like a fresh, brisk wind, draws me back to the truth and sets me and my small life in the greater context of God's person and purposes. Gratitude prepares me for soul searching under God's guidance and direction, not my own. Each day is a gift. There is a significant "Other," a giver and lover of my soul.

Sometimes it's easy to look back on a given day with gratitude. Just pausing to reflect brings to mind various blessings, conversations or "coincidences" that would otherwise have been lost to history. It feels natural to remember, to acknowledge, to look back and say, "This was a day the Lord made, I will rejoice and be glad in it!"

At other times, though, choosing gratitude is an act of faith. In particularly painful or confusing seasons of life, gratitude dries up. Even then, God is with us. "Even though I walk through the darkest valley, I will fear no evil," claims the psalmist. Why? Because there is no real threat? No. *For you are with me* (Psalm 23:4). God's presence really did accompany you throughout that day—as threatening or evil as the day may have been—whether you realized it or not. Perhaps just that reassurance will form the foundation of your gratitude today.

■ How naturally have you experienced gratitude toward God lately?

■ What do you think contributes to your current level of gratitude, whether high or low?

James 1:17 reminds us that every good and perfect gift is from above—from God. But the context of this verse gives us an important clue as to why we lose sight of this fact. The verse beforehand warns, "Don't be deceived, my dear brothers and sisters." Have you ever wondered *why* we are urged not to be deceived? I'm guessing it must be because we are prone to think otherwise—prone to be deceived in some way.

■ What does our world, or our culture, tell us that would stand in conflict with James 1:17?

■ Think about your own life. What deception might you believe, even today?

■ Take a moment, right now, to look back on your previous day with gratitude. It might help to write out a simple sentence or two, directed toward God, expressing thankfulness for this day.

Ask for Help from the Holy Spirit

This may seem obvious, but the third step in soul searching—again, before we ever get to the guts of reviewing the actual day—is to specifically *ask for help*. Often, we depend on our own resources even when they are in low supply. We struggle with dependence. That's why this step is so important.

Our previous steps were to recall that God is with us and to look back on the day with gratitude, but both of these steps can be done with God still at a bit of a distance. He could be a well-wisher, perhaps, standing near us at the airport gate—maybe even flying standby—before our flight into soul searching begins. But in this important step, we invite God to be the pilot, and we take a seat in coach.

Again, this may seem quite obvious during a prayer of examen. We are praying, after all! Shouldn't we assume the Holy Spirit will be involved? Yet the specific request for God's leadership matters. The explicit surrender of one's own leadership to the guidance of God prepares us and invites God's direct involvement.

If any of you lacks wisdom, you should ask God, who gives generously to all without finding fault, and it will be given to you. (James 1:5)

Ask and it will be given to you . . . for everyone who asks receives. (Matthew 7:7-8)

■ Use the following space to express your request for help from the Holy Spirit—not just in the prayer of examen, but in general! Also, see if you can sense your level of confidence that God will in fact answer your request. Speak with God about that as well.

Now we arrive at the "guts" of the prayer of examen form of soul searching.

Review Your Day

With God's guidance, look over your day scene by scene. John Ortberg has compared this to athletes who watch game films with their coach, noting the successes and failures of their performance in the game. The point of the exercise is not judgment or commendation, but rather learning and developing your relationship with the coach. The good news for us is that we can actually resolve the things we discover that were left undone or need to be rectified. But that's part of our final step—yet to come. For now, let's explore some questions to discern your actions and awareness of God throughout the day:

- When did I fail? *(Did you keep your word? Give your best effort? Did you cross a moral line? Ignore someone you could have helped?)*

- When did I love? *(Did you encourage one who was discouraged? Pray for someone? Pitch in to help someone with a project? Give someone else the better parking space? Extend forgiveness and compassion?)*

- Do I observe any habits or life patterns? *(Are you overeating? Shading the truth? Chronically late? Making excuses? Throwing a fit when you don't get your way?)*

- Have I seen both the positive and negative? *(We all have both!)*

- When did I see evidence of God's presence? *(Did you receive an answer to prayer? Wisdom for a decision? Comfort during a time of pain?)*

Perhaps just reading these questions brought to mind instances from your own life. Keep in mind that as we practice this form of soul searching, we don't enter these questions alone. We examine ourselves only after recalling we're in God's presence, looking back on the day with gratitude, and asking for divine guidance and help from the Holy Spirit.

Reconcile and Resolve

The final step in a prayer of examen brings closure to the experience, with an explicit focus on the future.

The philosopher Socrates reminds us of the futility in leading an unexamined life: "The unexamined life is not worth living." But why? Only when we consider our ways, when we become mindful of choices, of patterns, of mistakes and of blessings can we make wise choices for the future. The proverbs similarly advise, "The prudent see danger and take refuge, / but the simple keep going and pay the penalty" (Proverbs 27:12).

If we don't take the time to look, we may not notice the danger that lies ahead in our current course of action. Changing direction may mean any number of things, so this final portion of the classical prayer of examen guides us to consider exactly what.

For example, as various events of the day come to your awareness, God may direct you to a next step. Sharing the psalmist's request to "lead me in the way everlasting," you may feel led to return to a conversation with a loved one, just to check in on how they felt—perhaps you were a bit short with them or insensitive or impatient or dishonest or downright mean.

No matter what, the prayer of examen enables you to recognize an offense and move back toward the relationship in a spirit of contrition. It may be that you discover your own hurt feelings during a conversation or as a result of someone else's decision. In this case, your "resolve" step will be to confront the problem or otherwise deal with the hurt.

This step also provides opportunity for you to express your desires to God about the future. Perhaps you will be led to a time of confession, or of thanksgiving, or of surrender or resolve to a future course of action. The writer of Psalm 73 does this. Having spent time in reflection, the psalmist declares, "I will tell of all your deeds" (Psalm 73:28).

Psalm 73 offers a curious window into the "before and after" of an examen of sorts. The psalm begins with a lament over the apparent prosperity of the wicked, leaving the writer feeling self-pity over his seemingly wasted devotion to God: "As for me, my feet had almost slipped; / I had nearly lost my foothold. / For I envied the arrogant / when I saw the prosperity of the wicked" (vv. 2-3). The turning point comes in verse 17, when his perspective is entirely changed through an encounter with God—an encounter that sheds new light on his attitude and perspective. He says, "When I tried to understand all this, / it troubled me deeply / till I entered the sanctuary of God; / then I understood their final destiny" (vv. 16-17). As a result, he vows to tell of God's great deeds. It is a resolve that emerges from his experience of God enlightening his perspective.

Time for Examen

Take some extended time to move through each of these five steps right now. Ideally, you should have about ten to twenty minutes of un-interrupted time in order to move through this soul-searching prayer.

1. Recall you are in the presence of God.

2. Look at your day with gratitude.

3. Ask for help from the Holy Spirit.

4. Review your day.

5. Reconcile and resolve.

When Jacob awoke from his sleep, he thought, "Surely the Lord *is in this place, and I was not aware of it." (Genesis 28:16)*

I have found other helpful ways besides the classic prayer of examen to practice soul searching through my everyday life. One approach, a very simple review of the day, uses an outline to help us remember what happened the day before. Sometimes that's my first prayer: *Help me remember yesterday!*

For this simple review, I write out the specific activities of my day on the left-hand side of a page—what I did in the morning, what I worked on, who I had lunch or meetings with, etc. Once I've recorded the actual events, I return to each portion and prayerfully consider what my awareness of God was like during that piece of the day. I write my sense of God's presence and my receptivity to his promptings or guidance on the right-hand side of the page, opposite the events of that part of the day.

For example, maybe I was mindful of God's presence with me as I woke up that morning and was therefore eager for the day to unfold. But then I realize that during a ten o'clock meeting about a stressful project, I wasn't aware of God at all. Perhaps I responded defensively to someone's criticism or tried to bulldoze my way through someone else's concerns, both of which I now wish I had paid attention to. In the afternoon, someone might have called—like today—and reminded me of God's activity, causing my awareness to rise again. Of course, God never actually leaves us at any time—what changes is our consciousness of him!

As you review each of the main activities of the prior day, God helps you see patterns of openness. You may discover, over time, that being with certain people tends to elevate your awareness of God. Or you may notice that when you're involved in certain situations or engaged with specific people, your awareness of God just evaporates. You might even realize that most of the day went by before you truly connected with God, or even that you never connected with God at all! That's okay. Even just the process of noticing, under God's guidance, helps you grow.

This practice alone helps you cultivate the in-the-moment, real-time awareness of God. Over time, you can expect to see more and more of the right-hand side of a simple review page be overwhelmed by the presence of God! You will experience growth in your ability to truly abide in Christ, the way a graft branch remains in the central vine in order to live: "I am the vine; you are the branches. If you remain in me and I in you, you will bear much fruit; apart from me you can do nothing" (John 15:5).

Get the general idea? It really is fairly simple. Take the space on the following page to do your own review of the day using this outline, and perhaps you too will find that it helps with this form of soul searching. Don't forget to listen for God's direction as you prayerfully think through yesterday. This is not just self-analysis!

Day's events	My awareness of and responsiveness to God
Morning:	
Midday:	
Late afternoon:	
Evening:	
Bedtime	

Now that you've done the review, here are a few questions to consider.

■ What did you discover about your day?

■ Did you find something for which to be grateful? Anything that brings a tinge of regret?

■ Did you learn anything about yourself or God by doing this?

■ What do you think might happen if you did this practice on a regular basis?

As you practice the simple-review form of soul searching, you embrace your identity as a seeker—someone seeking a growing, real-time connection with God.

"Then you will call on me and come and pray to me, and I will listen to you. You will seek me and find me when you seek me with all your heart. I will be found by you," declares the Lord. *(Jeremiah 29:12-14)*

5 GROUP DISCUSSION

Summary

Spiritual leaders have long noticed the correlation between self-reflective prayer and ongoing, authentic spiritual transformation. Soul searching aimed at increasing our awareness of God can take a variety of forms, from the classical prayer of examen to a simple review of the day, or even writing in a journal about yesterday. But each of these methods draws us to some key steps: inviting God to lead our thoughts, often reflecting with gratitude on the gift of our day, and then investigating the specific episodes of a day, seeking an awareness of God's presence with us even as we develop our ability to connect with God during the prayer itself. We also pause to consider next steps on the basis of what we've discovered through the Holy Spirit's guidance. Even here, God leads the process, but we intentionally acknowledge his continuing leadership by specifically asking for guidance and direction. Over time, as we become more aware of God's presence in the past, we also become more aware of God's presence with us in the here and now. And greater awareness aids our ability to listen and hear from God in our daily activities, allowing us to really live in *relationship* with God.

Opening

What's something that almost always draws your attention back to God (a sunset, a child's laugh, a Scripture verse, beauty, the desperate needs in our world)?

Discussion

1. What, if anything, did you sense God stirring in you through this second experience?

2. Go back over your written responses to parts one through four. What one or two ideas stand out as something you'd like to bring to the group? Why did they stand out to you?

3. How did you respond to the story of Martha and Mary in Luke 10:38-42?

   What distractions pose the greatest threat to your paying attention to Jesus these days?

4. When you look back on ordinary days, do you tend to look back with regret and frustration or with gratitude?

What's something you can share with the group that you were grateful for just today? How did you see God's hand involved in that area?

5. What did you learn about yourself and about your relationship with God as you went through the review and resolve stages of the prayer of examen?

6. Read Jeremiah 29:12-14 out loud. How do God's words in these verses encourage you today? How do they challenge you?

Prayer

Have one or several group members close this time in prayer.

Before the next gathering, everyone should complete "Experience Three: Increasing Awareness of Self."

"The knowledge of ourselves not only arouses us to seek God, but also, as it were, leads us by the hand to find him."

JOHN CALVIN

EXPERIENCE THREE / *Increasing Awareness of Self*

1 **EXAMEN OF CONSCIENCE**

The overall idea of soul searching, in any form, is to identify and help remove barriers to a growing relationship with God. The examen of consciousness particularly identifies barriers of *inattentiveness* to God. As we have learned, the helpfulness of this practice stems from its ability to increase our capacity for experiencing God's presence in daily life. Naturally, increased awareness builds a deepening relationship!

Lack of awareness of God, though, is not the only thing that would threaten our spiritual health and growth. Our own actions and choices—both unintentional and intentional, small and large—can block our connection with God (separate us from him) and stymie our growth.

First Thessalonians 5:19 warns us that we, as believers, should not quench the Spirit's fire within us. What does that mean? What is it that would quench God's very life and activity in us? The short word is *sin:* our turning away from God and God's ways.

■ Getting more specific and personal, what things tend to have the greatest ability to quench the Spirit's fire within you?

■ What helps you notice times when you've turned away from God? Does it happen right away? Or take a long time?

What does "sin" look like?

The Bible presents sin by way of major concepts . . . expressed in an array of images: sin is the missing of a target, a wandering from the path, a straying from the fold. Sin is a hard heart and a stiff neck. Sin is blindness and deafness. It is both the overstepping a line and the failure to reach it—both transgression and shortcoming. Sin is a beast crouching at the door. In sin, people attack or evade or neglect their divine calling. These and other images suggest deviance: even when it is familiar, sin is never normal. Sin is disruption of created harmony and the resistance to divine restoration of that harmony. Above all, sin disrupts and resists the vital human relation to God, and it does all this disrupting and resisting in a number of intertwined ways.

(*Cornelius Plantinga Jr.,* Not the Way It's Supposed to Be)

Sometimes we're aware when we've turned, other times we're not. We are so easily deceived, and we conveniently forget. But whenever we prefer and choose our own way, we face the inevitable consequences, including our chosen separation from God. Soul searching helps us notice when and where we're disconnected from God—and it helps point the way back to a growing, restored relationship with him through confession and repentance.

Though tightly aligned, confession and repentance do differ slightly. Confession's focus centers on truth—on reality—and specifically on the incidents where we failed and are personally guilty, or culpable, for that failure. Confession admits personal wrongdoing; it takes personal ownership of sin.

Moving one step beyond personal responsibility, repentance speaks directionally. If, in the past, we were moving away from God (in one direction), then repentance signifies a turning back toward God. Repentance usually involves confession coupled with the energy of motion and a vector of new direction. In confession, we may well stand quite still though, significantly, we take ownership. In repentance, we also turn around.

Again, these ideas are closely linked, and both are essential in transformation. In ordinary life, however, they often move together almost seamlessly. We'll take a deeper look at both confession and repentance in experience four, but it's important to have them in mind as we raise our awareness of our self and our sin.

■ When did you first experience a true repentance in your relationship with God?

What brought you to that point?

■ When was a more recent time you experienced the distance that comes in relationship with God when we turn, even slightly, away?

Did you experience repentance? What happened?

In the next few sessions we'll explore different ways to practice examen of conscience, this aspect of soul searching that helps us learn to recognize the places and ways we're turning away from God.

One classic framework for soul searching references the fruit of the Spirit as identified in Galatians 5. The metaphor of fruit reinforces the concept that each of these virtues results as an outflow of something else—namely the life of God's Spirit having sway in our hearts and souls. When the human soul is moved along by the power and person of God, these qualities become increasingly evident.

Thus, it can be helpful to directly consider the degree of their presence or absence in our lives as an indicator of soul health. As God leads and directs the soul-searching process, we gain awareness regarding what's true—what's actually occurring in our lives—and what's not.

The concept of fruit extends beyond Galatians to several other biblical images, all of which have a common emphasis on seeing evidence of the interior state of the soul.

Consider the opening verses of Psalm 1, for instance:

Blessed are those
who do not walk in step with the wicked
or stand in the way that sinners take
or sit in the company of mockers,
but who delight in the law of the Lord

and meditate on his law day and night.
They are like a tree planted by streams of water,
    which yields its fruit in season
and whose leaf does not wither—
    whatever they do prospers.

Consider also Jesus' words of warning against those who pretend to lead but whose actions demonstrate a self-seeking:

Likewise, every good tree bears good fruit, but a bad tree bears bad fruit. A good tree cannot bear bad fruit, and a bad tree cannot bear good fruit. . . . Thus, by their fruit you will recognize them. (Matthew 7:17-18, 20)

The evidence of fruit in our lives, particularly the fruit of the Spirit, is something we can and should pay attention to, but we must be careful in our examination. An overemphasis on exterior evidence can lead to legalism, which Jesus soundly condemns earlier in Matthew 7 because it swiftly extinguishes an authentic spiritual life.

So what evidence should we look for? The evidence that creeps into everyday conversations and circumstances. It's easy to miss, easier still to ignore. That's why a direct approach—an intentional time of soul searching—can really aid spiritual growth and life.

Have you ever realized that it has been a long time since you felt true joy? Or have you ever wondered what authentic love (not arm-twisted-because-you-ought-to love) would be like? Have you noticed at any point that self-control is growing, not because of direct effort to control the self, but simply in a season of deep soul health? Perhaps you were surprised when peace or goodness or kindness sprang up during a time of conflict.

Most scholars agree that the fruits listed in Galatians 5 are really all about love. Perhaps a more accurate reading of the text would have punctuation to clarify the emphasis on love—maybe something like this:

The fruit (singular noun) of the Spirit is love: joy, peace, patience, kindness, goodness, faithfulness, gentleness and self-control.

Each of the additional fruits named can be thought of as *ways* that love gets lived out in relationship. If the greatest commandment is to love God and love others, then we can assume each of these fruits have their fruition (so to speak) in relationships: Peace in relationship with others (not just on a beach by yourself). Kindness toward the marginalized, or toward those who have hurt us. Goodness to rectify wrongs, to make things "good" in issues like social justice or even concern for the environment. Self-control to curb the tendency to say or do hurtful things to others (not to pride ourselves in a highly regimented life).

Prayerfully consider each of these, asking God to reveal where the fruit of the Spirit has been present or absent in you. You may find this leads to a time of deeper soul searching to understand what has helped or hindered the activity of God. I hope you'll be both challenged and encouraged by what you discover.

■ Where has the fruit of the Holy Spirit been either present or absent in my life this week? Respond to God in the space provided for each of the characteristics listed.

Love:

Joy:

Peace:

Patience:

Kindness:

Goodness:

Faithfulness:

Gentleness:

Self-Control:

3 SEVEN DEADLY SINS

Some find it helpful in their soul searching to prayerfully review what are known as the seven deadly sins: pride, envy, gluttony, lust, anger, greed and sloth. Originally, these vices were identified to place some framework around the darkest parts of the human nature—the parts most inclined to live in refusal of the person and place of God in our lives. Pride has often been thought to be the root, even, of all the others because pride represents an ultimate refusal to acknowledge God as God.

Here are some definitions for each of these sins.*

- Pride is understood to be the sin of Satan, expressed in his desire to be like God. Pride wants to focus attention anywhere but on its own sinfulness and does not concede that Christ has any authority to condemn our sinfulness.

- Envy is dissatisfaction with who God has made me to be. It is also suspicion that God is withholding what I deserve and giving it to someone else.

- Gluttony is the pursuit and overindulgence of the body's appetites, especially for food and drink.

---

*Taken and adapted from *Signature Sins* by Michael Mangis (Downers Grove, Ill.: IVP Books, 2008).

- Lust has its root in the belief that God's love is not enough to satisfy our longing for intimacy and seeks to fill that longing through visual and physical sexual sin.

- Anger that is inordinate or inappropriate (sinful) is directed at selfish and mundane matters. Sinful anger comes unbidden and in greater intensity than the situation warrants.

- Greed grows out of the suspicion that God will not take care of our needs as well as we can do it ourselves. It is oriented toward material possessions, wanting the good things that others have.

- Sloth is the neglect of the greatest commandment: to love the lord your God with all your heart, soul, mind and strength. It's inattention to our spiritual lives, and failure to do anything that God asks of us or even simply what needs to be done.

During a time of soul searching, you can simply jot down each of these sins in a notebook or journal, and then prayerfully ask God for his direction: Is there anything God might say to you regarding the effect of pride in your life? When did envy rear its ugly head recently? What provoked the envy, and how did you respond? How about gluttony? Overindulging seems to be the norm in modern society—what place does it have in your heart? How has it kept you from God? What shrivels in your soul when gluttony rules?

Get the idea? As you move through each of these seven vices, keep in mind that your goal is simply to allow this exercise to structure your conversation with God. Allow the Spirit of God to bring conviction where appropriate, but do not give in to condemnation at all!

■ Use the space below to do a soul-searching exercise reviewing the seven deadly sins.

Pride:

Envy:

Gluttony:

Lust:

Anger:

Greed:

Sloth:

By now you may be a bit overwhelmed by all this scrutiny! I hope not. My hope is that you have heard the voice of a loving and gentle Shepherd—One who loves you deeply, personally and relentlessly.

C. S. Lewis wrote in *The Four Loves* that the nature of love is to improve the object of its affection. Love is not content to leave the object of its devotion as is when as is brings heartbreak or frustration or danger. Love desires the best, the freest, the most-true-to-its-identity. Lewis argued that apathy, not hatred, is the opposite of love. Hatred still connects us to the person: we're angry, we've been hurt, we wish they were other than what they are. But true apathy is the opposite of love. We just don't care. We are unconcerned. We have severed the connection. The other person has become invisible to us.

That's why, when we really love someone, we naturally begin to care about their spiritual development and long for them to become all that God intends. Too often, though, we eventually lose sight of what's best and become obsessed with perfection and performance. Most of us have been on the receiving end of a relationship like this; probably most of us have also been on the giving side as well. In relationship with God, however, his loving concern for what's best never changes.

God's pure love is not withheld even one shred when we fail or fall short or refuse to follow.

I suspect that when we fail, God most actively pursues us. Not as a fussy, uptight perfectionist, but as a shepherd who leaves everything behind just to find the one sheep who is lost. As a woman who relentlessly scrounges for a treasured possession. As a tender-hearted, lavish and forgiving father who patiently, expectantly waits for the day we come to our senses and turn back home.

■ Have you received much "love that wants the best" in human relationships? Or have your relationships been characterized more by conditional love?

■ How do you generally expect to be received by the current relationships in your life when you fail?

■ How do you expect to be received by God?

Many of us naturally avoid anything that exposes our darkness, sometimes because we have been deeply wounded by those who could not handle our shortcomings, much less lovingly point us to God. We've been crushed and broken for our flaws, shamed for our faults, hated for our failures. We were not received or forgiven or healed. So after years of defending ourselves from blows and attacks, it takes a long time of trust-building with God to lay down the armor of self-protection carefully placed around our soul. Most of us have a hard time even imagining living that openly, that undefended, in our relationship with God. But eventually we can come to trust what the beloved disciple John knew to be true: "There is no fear in love. But perfect love drives out fear, because fear has to do with punishment" (1 John 4:18).

Even with God's guidance helping us search out our soul, we feel the sting of pain over our faults. For some of us, that sting is rooted in fear of punishment, abandonment, rejection or more. But if we could imagine, for a moment, that those fears were set aside, enabling us to face our shortcomings without fear, my guess is we still might feel a sting.

What's that sting? Some call it guilt; some call it shame. Guilt is feeling bad about *what I did or did not do*. The focus is outside the self, aimed at a decision, an action, an omission.

Shame, though, is much deeper. Shame enters my life when I feel bad about *who I am*. No longer at a distance, shame creeps into every fiber of my being. Shame is not about what I did; it points inside to who I am. It's a terrible burden to bear. That's why I love it at church when our pastors remind us—making the fresh appeal to those far from God—that Jesus removes both our guilt and our shame.

There are different kinds of shame, though. *Deserved shame* is what we feel when we've done something wrong and realize it's because we are that kind of person. Lewis Smedes points this out in his helpful work *Shame and Grace.*

Shame, we are told, is the painful feeling of being a flawed human being. Well, what if, in fact, we are flawed human beings? All of us. Cracked vessels. Wheels out of alignment. The heart of us slightly off center. What if none of us is quite a match for the self we could be?

Given the horrors that some of our species consistently inflict on others, why should we blame our shame? Why should we not be thankful that we still have the power to feel it? Given the crabbed side of my own spirit, my irresistible urge to seek my own interests at the expense of others, my comfort in the teeth of other people's suffering, my [cowardly] envy at other people's success, and given my urges to smash the nose of any driver who cuts in front of me, given such flaws, am I not more in tune with reality if I accept my shame as the cost of failing to be the self I ought to be, the self I am meant to be, the self I really want to be? This is healthy shame, and we are closest to health when we let ourselves feel the pain of it and be led by the pain to do something about it.

If I never feel shame, I have become either totally divine or totally corrupt—and my best intuitions tell me I am neither. (p. 34)

It must be noted, though, that while legitimate reasons for shame lurk in our souls, many people—far too many—carry *undeserved shame* because they suffered some type of abuse (whether emotional, physical, verbal or sexual). Often the shame is so deep, so long-standing, that they hardly know themselves without it. Their shame has become their identity. How desperately these people need freedom! It's one thing to be held captive by our own foolishness. It's another thing entirely to become imprisoned at the hands of another. Freedom is still available in Christ, though the process of healing is different.

The loudest and most insistent voices of shame often fall in that undeserved category, Smedes notes, through *culture* (constant reinforcement that you are not enough), *graceless religion* (if you follow the rules, you are acceptable; otherwise, you are not) or *unaccepting parents* (your earliest sense of self and value). And unfortunately, these sources of undeserved shame so dominate our emotional landscape that we can easily miss the occasional sources of deserved shame that may coexist in that realm.

■ Think through your relationship to those powerful voices of undeserved shame. To which are you most susceptible? Why?

■ How might these sources of undeserved shame impact your ability to sense deserved shame (the healthy kind that Lewis Smedes described)?

■ Take some time to speak with God directly about your shame. Perhaps a new season of intense healing may open up to you as you become increasingly free from all forms of shame.

■ Read Isaiah 61 in its entirety. Read it again, quite slowly. What do you sense God saying to you, or emphasizing, if anything?

If soul searching seems to provoke feelings of undeserved shame in your life, it might be best to focus only on the forms of soul searching that examine our consciousness of God until those soul wounds have been significantly healed. A wise mentor, friend or spiritual director could possibly help guide you in this process.

5 GROUP DISCUSSION

Summary

Sometimes soul searching takes the form of a prayerful but direct exploration of our conscience, echoing the cry of the psalmist, "See if there is any offensive way in me, / and lead me in the way everlasting." No matter how long we've been in a relationship with God, each of us still wrestles with a dimension of our personhood that resists or refuses God and his ways. When we give in to those temptations, we turn away from God's love and life. Sometimes we realize it, and sometimes we don't. Turning back, or repenting, is just a natural part of an ongoing healthy spiritual life. Soul searching can help us stay healthy by periodically looking within to see if and how we have strayed. Helpful frameworks such as the fruit of the Spirit or the seven deadly sins can provide some structure to guide our prayers, but the central focus always remains: allow God to lead. In this way, we allow his light to penetrate even the darkest places of our souls and simultaneously receive that same light as a source of forgiveness, grace and healing. Thus, an examination of the conscience need not be feared. With God leading the process, we are not crushed by deserved shame nor threatened by undeserved shame. Instead, we receive new life and unconditional love that aids our spiritual growth and development, helping us become more like Christ.

Opening

How do you respond to the statement "Ignorance is bliss"? Do you agree or disagree? Why?

Discussion

1. What, if anything, did you sense God stirring in you through this third experience?

2. Go back over your written responses to parts one through four. What one or two ideas stand out as something you'd like to bring to the group? Why did they stand out to you?

3. Talk about your personal stories of repentance, both past and present, from the opening questions of part one.

4. What was your experience of soul searching like when using the fruit of the Spirit as a guide? What did you learn? What was difficult? Confusing? Encouraging?

5. What stood out to you in the exercise reviewing the seven deadly sins?

6. Read Romans 8:1-2 out loud. How well does this verse match your experience as a Christian?

   What might help you stay connected to the truth that there is *no condemnation* for you in Christ?

7. How could your group help each other live the reality of grace more often?

Prayer

Have one or several group members close this time in prayer.

Before the next gathering, everyone should complete "Experience Four: Responding to Grace."

"Grace must find expression in life,
otherwise it is not grace."

KARL BARTH

EXPERIENCE FOUR / *Responding to Grace*

1 EARLY DETECTION, EARLY CURE

Regardless of the format used in soul searching, an inevitable issue arises. Even if we successfully navigate to a place of contrition without shame or inordinate guilt, we're left to wonder, *What do we do with what we find?* My friend Aimee Mury's story inspires me about how we must answer this essential question of soul searching.

When Aimee was in first grade, she suffered the loss of her mother to a rare stomach cancer. Her mom was just thirty-three years old when she died. Aimee is now a mom herself, with three young children. Recently, Aimee and her family began to notice the very high rate of cancer in her extended family on her mother's side. They did some testing and discovered that she had a genetic predisposition to this cancer. The experts could not predict when, but with great certainty they confirmed that Aimee would eventually develop this aggressive, hard-to-detect stomach cancer. The physicians outlined her options for treatment and made their own recommendations. But of course, the final decision about *what to do with what they found* rested with Aimee. Considering not only her own fate but the lives of her children, Aimee and her husband, John, decided on a radical response to this finding: a complete stomach-ectomy. This surgical procedure, which completely removes the stomach, had rarely been done, and typically only in response to massive trauma. Though the surgery involved great risk and a very different postoperative lifestyle, the choice for Aimee was relatively easy. She wanted to live.

Aimee's choices help me see that I too have options when I face the cancers in my life. These are not physical cancers but the sneaky cancers of the soul—out-of-control areas of darkness that threaten to alter my vitality.

We can always ignore the dark threats, minimize them, try to work around them. Or, like Aimee, we can trust the advice of a wise Physician and surrender ourselves to a sin-ectomy: removing sin, so to speak, through the process of confession—calling sin what it is and bringing it out into the light so we can receive God's forgiveness and grace.

Keep in mind that confession is not a mere exercise in cosmic bookkeeping. It's not about keeping the "forces" in balance, as in Newton's third law of motion (every action has an equal and opposite reaction). Instead, confession is powerful soul leverage. Confession actually holds the potential to release us from the grip of destructive forces. Confession opens the door to transformation.

■ How was the idea of confession handled in your family of origin?

■ How about in a spiritual community you were involved in early on in your faith?

■ How is confession addressed or discussed in your current community?

■ How do you personally experience confession? When was the last time you had a sin-ectomy conversation with God? With someone you hurt?

After we genuinely confess our sin, it's time to repent: to turn back to God. If you remember from part one of experience three, confession and repentance are different from each other but work together closely. We can see each of them distinctly in this metaphor of Aimee's story. First, Aimee courageously *acknowledged the truth* of what was inside her (though of course it represented not a shred of personal guilt). Then, knowing the truth, she made a *change in direction*. For her in her physical awareness and us in our "sin awareness," not changing direction in light of the truth we've gained is almost unthinkable and certainly dangerous.

That's why her example—her courageous choice—is so inspiring to me, though I must face the disease within my own soul that does not reflect amoral genes but rather the dark cancerous forces of pride, deceit, jealousy, envy and the like, of which I am decidedly (and sometimes frequently) guilty.

Is it enough to merely notice them, even call them what they are, without also turning toward healing and grace? Soul searching helps both the process of identification leading to confession and the subsequent process of repentance. Of coming to believe there is a better way, in alignment with God, and then returning my will toward that direction.

From a spiritual perspective . . . no matter how much grace God has blessed us with, we forever remain dependent upon its continuing flow. (Gerald May, Addiction and Grace)

One of the best illustrations of the power of confession comes from a biblical metaphor often used to describe spiritual transformation: the refining of impure metals. Valuable metals such as gold, silver and platinum can get mixed with less valuable metals, either in their natural state or when used in products. These impure metals, whether naturally occurring ores or alloy mixtures, are purified by the process of refining. Today we have a variety of high-tech ways to refine metals, but in ancient times the process always involved subjecting the metal substance to heat—intense heat. Extreme temperatures cause the impurities enmeshed within the mixture to separate and rise to the surface, where they can be removed.

So what does this have to do with the soul? Look up these verses: Jeremiah 9:7, Zechariah 13:9, Malachi 3:3 and Proverbs 17:3.

■ How does the refining process connect to transformation?

The purification process in our lives works much the same way. Though we may have varying degrees of awareness of the impure tendencies within us, the fact is that when the heat gets turned up, these flaws come to the surface. When we are under duress or in painful, disappointing, confusing, difficult or trying times, the vices of jealousy, manipulation, striving, defensiveness, meanness and dozens of other impurities quickly rise to the surface. Usually, the higher the heat, the more obvious they are. Without the heat of hard times, their presence, while still weakening our strength and rendering us useless for certain tasks, remains mostly invisible When the heat gets turned up, however, the vices are exposed or expressed. There, at the surface of my life, I can see them. Others can see them.

I hate those parts of myself. I know them to be wrong or sinful—I know I shouldn't be envious or mean or manipulative. So what do I do when impurities come to the surface? Expending tremendous energy and fueled by my own pride, I work furiously to push them back down. I work very hard to not allow rage or anything impure to come to the surface. Unknowingly, I refuse the opportunity to be purified, to be transformed. I become a pretender, choosing weakness instead of growth.

When those things do come to the surface, my soul needs confession, not repression. If I choose to suppress them, those toxins will destroy my soul and those around me. But if I allow them to come to the surface as the heat gets turned up in my life, I can speak with God and sometimes with others about what has surfaced in me. And when I choose to expose those impurities, I walk not only in forgiveness but also with the firm hope of being made new. Little by little and day by day, newness is happening. Freedom is winning. Truth is winning. Righteousness is winning.

With that as our backdrop, let's look with fresh eyes at the way the apostle James urges his readers to trust in the connection between the "heat being turned up" and transformation:

Consider it pure joy, my brothers and sisters, whenever you face trials of many kinds, because you know that the testing of your faith produces perseverance. Let perseverance finish its work so that you may be mature and complete, not lacking anything. (James 1:2-4)

■ In what ways has the heat been turned up in your life?

■ When that happens, what have you noticed coming to the surface?

■ What have you been doing with impurities when they come to the surface?

■ In what ways have you seen past "heat" result in transformation?

Rewrite James 1:2-4 using the example of your own circumstances and growth. You can write this from the perspective of past trials that you now see helped cultivate strength of character, or—this will take great faith!—write about a current trial and the character you hope God may develop in you through this time.

Take the remaining space on this page to respond to God honestly about both your circumstances and God's process of refining.

Once I came to a friend asking for a chance to be heard on something I had deep regret over. It did not involve my friend, but I felt I needed to bring this area of struggle into the light and talk about it. As I recounted my choice and what, in hindsight, I felt had been wrong, she listened attentively. She then reminded me of God's forgiveness and the healing work that was advancing in my soul as a result of "coming clean."

As soon as she finished speaking her grace-and-truth-filled reminder to me, I began to assure her of my plans to make sure I never did that kind of thing again. Her experienced ears heard not only my words but also my deep self-hatred for the fact that I struggled with something so persistently frustrating, and my deep self-reliance for spiritual growth. She gently stopped me in the midst of my shrill resolves and offered a perspective hard-won through time spent in a twelve-step recovery program. Between our Diet Cokes in the booth where we sat, she wrote these three words on a napkin: *Awareness, Acceptance, Action*. What I learned that night has shaped my understanding of confession and opened me up to the process of transformation.

When we realize the error of our ways, under the guidance of the

Holy Spirit, we're at the *awareness* stage. We have become aware of our wrongdoing, or of something we should have done but didn't. Most often, we live in deep denial and blindness to the things we do that harm others, and when awareness comes it is painful. We may despise ourselves, hating that we were weak or selfish, or that the consequences of our choices have harmed ourselves, others and even God's reputation in the world. This, as we have said, is the sting of guilt and shame—some deserved, some not. But awareness is the first step in this three-part process. Awareness is what happens when our character defects come to the surface—when we *see* the impurity within us.

■ Take some time to write about an area that's been a personal struggle for you lately. (This should not be about what someone else has been doing wrong!)

■ What things (events, Scripture, conversations, promptings) have raised your awareness of this area in your life?

When we see the impurities that exist, we often reject them. (That's the pushing-it-back-down tendency.) Then, in order to prevent the wrongdoing from happening in the future (because we don't want to be *that kind of person*), we develop our plan of action. We invent ways to make sure it won't happen again. Naturally, of course, it still does. But in that moment, the intoxicating combination of pride and shame seduces us into thinking we can power our way into self-improvement. We leap from awareness to self-directed action. And rarely do such measures bring lasting change. If they do effect change, they equally reinforce the strength of pride and shame guiding us, and that will ultimately backfire. When we give our allegiance to pride and shame, we serve a relentless and harsh master.

The alternative—a new way to live—involves *acceptance*. Acceptance, in this context, does not mean accepting that our actions weren't really wrong. On the contrary, acceptance of this kind means accepting that I am *the kind of person* who did that, who does that. Certainly our failure in specific areas is not the only thing that's true about us, or even the defining truth of who we are. But it is the truth of who I am right now. I need to accept responsibility not only for the action or inaction itself but also for the fact that the action sprang forth from a person—me—and that somehow the choice made sense. If I want to heal, I need to accept that.

As my friend challenged me, I deeply resisted her words. And the longer I sat with my resistance, the more I could sense that my resistance was my pride. Acceptance in this case would mean laying down, once again, my self-righteousness.

But then I realized that acceptance would also open me up to grace. I apparently still resist being *the kind of woman* who actually needs grace. (Perhaps I think I'm above it? That I somehow qualified for the spiritual sufficiency club?) But rather than corralling my forces and ramping up my resolve, I need to let go and render myself helpless, insufficient, dependent and ready to receive God's grace.

■ Thinking back to your own situation, how have you responded to increasing awareness in your area of struggle?

■ What would acceptance mean for you in this area? (Remember, this is not an issue of condoning your actions, but rather owning them in a way that allows you to receive grace.)

■ Take some time to pray, specifically asking God to be with you in this area of your life. In this prayer, admit your need and inability to "power up" to self-improvement.

From that place of weakness, not false strength, I eventually do move to *action*. But the action is initiated by God. The action is directed by God. The action springs from an invitation God extends—an invitation to a different way. It may, in fact, be an action I would have chosen for myself, or it may be an entirely different next step. Either way, the process by which I come to that next step differs greatly, as will the outcome. As I allow God to lead and direct my next steps, my strength and power as a person of grace, unflinching truth, deep dependence and humility form in my inner person. These qualities are the very opposite of what develops when I bow my knee to pride and shame.

Can we really trust that God will, in fact, lead us? That's where King David landed after a time of soul searching: "Lead me in the way everlasting," he wrote in Psalm 139. When we acknowledge our inability to lead ourselves in the way everlasting, it makes infinite sense to ask for help from the One who can!

■ Is there an action step you know God is asking you to take in this area? What is it?

■ If you are willing, lay this area of your life, as best you can, on the altar of transformation. (See Romans 12:1-2.)

This, then, is our context as we move into soul searching the conscience directly:

- When the heat gets turned up in our lives, we can expect the impurities to rise to the surface.

- Soul searching aids awareness, helping us face those unsavory parts of ourselves that keep us stuck in destructive patterns.

- Resisting the temptation to force our impurities underneath the surface once again, we move into confession, not for the sake of bookkeeping but with the sure hope of transformation, freedom and life.

- With confession, we adopt a posture of acceptance—we actually *receive* the grace extended to us.

- Abandoning self-improvement strategies, we patiently wait in expectation and dependence for God to lead and guide us in next steps. And when he does, we take action.

Use the following questions (included all together here for easy access and reuse) for a guided solitude experience of soul searching around awareness, acceptance and action.

1. Take some time to write about an area that's been a personal struggle for you lately. (This should not be about what someone else has been doing wrong!)

2. What things (events, Scripture, conversations, promptings) have raised your awareness of this area in your life?

3. How have you responded to this increasing awareness?

4. What would acceptance mean for you in this area? (Remember, this is not an issue of condoning your actions, but rather owning them in a way that allows you to receive grace.)

5. Take some time to pray, specifically asking God to be with you in this area of your life. In this prayer, admit your need and inability to "power up" to self-improvement.

6. Is there an action step you know God is asking you to take in this area? What is it?

7. If you are willing, lay this area of your life, as best you can, on the altar of transformation.

Therefore, there is now no condemnation for those who are in Christ Jesus, because through Christ Jesus the law of the Spirit who gives life has set you free from the law of sin and death. (Romans 8:1-2)

As you develop the ability to periodically take an honest look inside, guided by the Holy Spirit, God will provide care and nurture for your soul. You will develop an increased capacity to experience God's leadership and direction in daily activities—moving into what the Quakers refer to simply as "guidance." While you may sense pangs of sadness or regret, I trust you will experience the powerful reality of hope—hope that God is *yet* at work in your life!

Over time, the paradox of spiritual life becomes your story, as it has been the story of many throughout the ages: parts of us die, and yet we are raised to new life. Through dying to the self, we become more closely aligned to the person God had in mind at our inception.

You will look in the mirror and truly recognize who's there. More and more every day, you can look straight at the darkest parts, and look directly into the light. Shoulders down, no pretense. God is God, you are not, and you are alive!

When should you take opportunity for soul searching as a way to care for your soul? Ignatius advised two formal times of examen each day, but that may not be practical for everyone.

At a minimum, we would be wise to heed the directive given in 1 Corinthians 11:28: "Everyone ought to examine themselves before they eat of the bread and drink of the cup." We should pause, even for a moment, to do a soul-searching exercise before participating in Communion. As we examine ourselves, we invite God to bring to our attention anything blocking our relationship; we ask for a purification of our motives. Jesus coveys a similar idea when he advises in the Sermon on the Mount, "Therefore, if you are offering your gift at the altar and there remember that your brother or sister has something against you, leave your gift there in front of the altar. First go and be reconciled to that person; then come and offer your gift" (Matthew 5:23-24).

On ordinary days, soul searching may take a variety of forms. Some may choose to review their lives on a daily basis using a format like the one described in experience two in this study, or by simply reflecting in the pages of a journal. I often lean into one or another format on the basis of what I sense my current need to be. At other times, I sense I am just skimming the surface of my own life, missing the bigger picture. It's as if I'm wearing earmuffs—I can't hear much, and things around me begin to look absurd. When I feel the deafness coming on, I often commit to a season of more intentional soul searching using the Ignatian prayer of examen.

■ What are your typical, daily rhythms for caring for your soul?

How might the various means of soul searching that you've learned in this study affect those times in the future?

■ Remember the object you chose in experience one as a symbol of your desire to raise your awareness of God (p. 17)? Look at it or pick it up. Talk with God about why you chose the object or picture you did. Let that symbolic object also serve as a reminder to you of your need for soul searching, and the deeper connection to God that comes out of it.

Soul searching with a structure such as the fruit of the Spirit, the seven deadly sins or even the Ten Commandments would ideally be incorporated into a longer period of time, maybe even during a retreat experience where extended time for reflection is already in place. It's hard to hear God's voice directing a sensitive conversation if we are hurried or apt to be interrupted. I would also suggest bringing a soul friend or other spiritual adviser into the process. Perhaps they can pray for you during your retreat; most likely they will be glad, and humbled, to hear your "confession" if you feel led to speak with someone in addition to God. Most important, they can remind you of your identity as a loved, treasured, pursued and in-process child of God.

■ When in the near future do you have time to set aside for solitude and reflection?

■ Who could you recruit to pray for you during that time, and how might you prepare them in advance for the option of coming alongside you in your refining process?

■ What practical and tangible item—perhaps one that you can carry with you, or at least that you'll see every day—could serve to remind you of your truest identity in Christ, as one who is fully loved, fully accepted and free to walk joyfully over the earth?

5 GROUP DISCUSSION

Summary

Caring for your soul through times of intentional soul searching is like the process of allowing a wise physician to see the truth about a physical danger (like cancer) lurking in your body, and then dealing with it in order to bring freedom and life. It's easy to trust a physical doctor who may recommend a particular course of action, but when it comes to the soul, we aren't always as willing to be led. Our human perspective, however, flawed and limited as it is, will not be a trustworthy guide in matters of the soul. Sometimes we're tempted to ignore or push back down whatever God reveals, but this can thwart the essential refining process in which the junk of our lives comes to the surface so that it can be removed. When the truth about our interior world does come out, we need to ask, *What do we do with what we find?* We might be tempted to pursue a course of action apart from God's loving wisdom, direction and guidance. Here again, if our prideful ego steps in to take control, it could seriously derail the process God has for us. Rather, we must wait on God. We must listen for the still, small voice of our powerful but gentle Savior—one who can be fully trusted with our eternity, and also with this very moment.

Opening

When have you had to face a hard truth about your physical health (or the health of someone you love)?

Discussion

1. What, if anything, did you sense God stirring in you through this fourth experience?

2. Go back over your written responses to parts one through four. What one or two ideas stand out as something you'd like to bring to the group? Why did they stand out to you?

3. Talk a bit about your personal journey as it relates to confession (questions from part one). When did you first learn about confession from the Bible? What form does confession take (or what form has it taken in the past) in your life?

4. Look up and read each of the verses on refining in part two. How have you seen this process at work in your life in the past? Recently?

5. What did you learn in part three by pausing, between awareness and action, to consider acceptance?

6. How can your group pray for you as you complete this study?

Prayer
Take some extended time for prayer during this final group time. Spend a few minutes praying specifically for each person and for their ability to sense God's presence and to respond willingly to God's loving leadership in their lives.

CONCLUSION
No More Stains

November 4

Yesterday . . .

I spent an unbelievable amount of money having the carpets and couches cleaned yesterday. Everything *was treated with Scotchguard and deodorizer. God, I am sorry if this was unwise, but we've had couches for twelve or thirteen years that have never been cleaned—they've been dumped on, thrown up on, etc., so I felt it best to do it all at the same time to get the best price. So I just did it. Everything.*

But the shocker, and I do mean shocker, has been this: the stains are gone. Stains that have lived through the last two cleanings by the same company (a new team, they claim, is the reason) are gone. I have white carpet once again! I'm nervous that somehow this morning, I'll see them all again. But even if just for one night (and I hope it's not!), I found You speaking through these sparkling carpets. I know exactly where each of those familiar old stains rested—every puppy misdemeanor I've noticed dozens of times literally every day, red wine up the stairs, polka-dots in the boy's bedroom and office. Stain after stain after stain. Over the years, they just became part of the domestic landscape—ugly, unkempt and a bit gross.

And now they are gone.

On the floors, at least for now, there is beauty, order and uniformity. And I actually discover that my focus is drawn to what really matters in the home—people and work and conversations and snuggles. I am not distracted, and internally repulsed, by the stains.

I keep hearing You say, "Notice." I wonder, why? Why do you want me to see how clean this is?

Eventually, I sense You conveying a message—about how naturally I come to accept and live with various stains on my soul. Ugly, unkempt and a little gross, they stand as silent reminders of damage I've done, or of damage done to me, whether misdemeanors or felonies. The destructive events themselves have been absorbed in history, but the stains remain, ugly and gross.

I hear You saying, "Notice. Notice what the 'freedom' from old stains looks like. You can be stain-free too."

Thank you, Jesus, for removing my soul stains just as completely as the stains in my carpet. Please grant me freedom from constantly noticing and remembering the evidence, the damage, the proof *of former soul stains. Let me live with newfound freedom to focus on what matters most—people and work and conversations and snuggles. Please lead and guide me today, please heal and empower, please love me and let me love You.*

That was a recent journal entry for me during a time of soul searching and listening. I included the entry not necessarily as a how-to for soul searching, but rather to bring us back to where we began—our identity. I hope that through this process you've begun to see that your identity is a mixed bag. Great virtues coexist with great vices, and they all swirl around together in the cauldron of everyday life. Yet as God loves us and draws us deeper into relationship, the process of refining is an expression of God's love and of his intentionality for our lives. There are important relationships and important actions that God has in mind for your life. You need the character to match that assignment, and so do I, so into the refiner's fire we go!

Soul searching helps you embrace this process and receive God's gifts of grace and transformation. You're in the process of becoming the truest *you*—a forgiven, in-process person. The person God intends for you to be.

I hope that when you next look into a mirror, your eyes won't dart askance in shame or widen with pride. Instead, I hope your eyes will look with a steady gaze of honor, compassion, mercy and grace on a forgiven and deeply loved child of our great God. Walk away from that mirror with a quiet confidence, knowing now with even greater clarity both who you are and, most important, Whose you are.

ALSO AVAILABLE IN SOUL CARE® RESOURCES

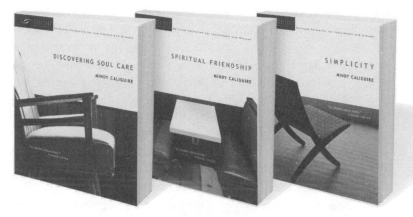

Discovering Soul Care
978-0-8308-3509-6

Spiritual Friendship
978-0-8308-3510-2

Simplicity
978-0-8308-3522-5

To connect with Mindy Caliguire
and learn more about the SoulCare ministry
visit <www.soulcare.com>.